People of Choice

"Live a life where assumptions don't rule your truth."

People of Choice

Written by **Divya**

Published on: June 1, 2025
First Edition
ISBN: 978-93-343-0669-9
Cover Design: Aarav
Published by: Self-Published
Contact: ntgistoo@gmail.com

This book is a work of self-reflection and emotional exploration. Any resemblance to actual events or persons, living or dead, is purely coincidental unless otherwise noted.

Dedication

To my brother,
Ajay Kumar Vincent,
whose unwavering support and encouragement have been my guiding light.

And to my love,
Vinay Kumar,
who shows me that love can explore beyond boundaries, inspiring me to dream, grow, and believe in the beauty of the journey.

CONTENTS

INTRODUCTION

This book is not here to teach you how to become someone else. It's here to remind you—you can choose to become more of yourself.

We all go through life wearing layers of boldness, silence, overthinking, over-giving, and sometimes, pretending. We speak less, feel more. We love deeply, yet often without clarity. We hurt, we hold, and we hide. But at the end of every story, every relationship, every moment of struggle, there is a choice. And that choice is always yours.

People of Choice is not a book filled with rules or instructions. It is not about becoming perfect. It's about becoming aware. About noticing the difference between reacting and responding. Between acting strong and being strong. Between loving unconsciously and loving with truth.

In these pages, you'll find a conversation—a mirror. A space where I've poured my experiences, my love journey, my breakdowns, and my growth. It's not written from the top of a mountain but from the middle of the path—just like yours. I have loved and lost. I have chosen pain, peace, silence, and honesty. And every time I did, I discovered that freedom was not in avoiding emotions, but in facing them.

This book is for the overthinker who wants peace.
For the quiet one who wants to speak.
For the lover who's unsure whether to stay or let go.
For anyone who's ever wanted to feel **seen**, not fixed.

You don't need to agree with every word. You only need to reflect. If even one page brings you back to yourself, makes you pause, makes you choose—you've already begun.

This isn't about becoming someone new.
It's about **returning to you.**

Let's begin.

— *With truth, awareness, and love,*
DIVYA MADHABATTULA
Author of *People of Choice*

PART ONE
The Battle Within by Thinking

Chapter 1: Choose Your Feelings and Emotions

Emotions vs. Feelings

For a long time, I believed that emotions and feelings were the same. That's what I felt was automatically real and valid, because I felt it. But the more I watched myself react, stay quiet, or even smile through emotional noise, I began to question: What am I actually feeling—and what am I carrying without awareness?

[“Emotions are automatic, physical responses triggered by the brain in reaction to a situation. Feelings are the conscious experience of emotions. You see a snake → your body reacts with fear (emotion) → you think “I’m scared” (feeling).”]

I remember sitting silently in rooms where I was supposed to feel hurt, but I didn’t. And still, I told myself, “You should feel bad. You should cry. You should react.” But why?

Because somewhere along the way, I had learned to match the situation, not my truth. I confused expectation with emotion.

That's when I first realized: Emotions happen to you, but feelings are what you allow to stay. Emotions are the raw storm—automatic, fast, sometimes protective. But feelings? Feelings are chosen. They're the meaning you hold onto after the emotion has passed.

✧ A Moment That Taught Me

I had a best friend who was emotionally close to me—we shared everything. But one day, without any explanation, she suddenly stopped talking to me. The emotion hit me like a wave. I felt rejected. Confused. Maybe even a little angry. But instead of drowning in those emotions, I paused. I breathed. And I told myself: "What if this isn't about me? What if she's going through something I don't know?" In that moment, I chose understanding over self-pity. I chose to hold space instead of hurt. And to my surprise, that choice brought peace. I felt light, not heavy. I felt connected, not abandoned, because I didn't let assumptions rule my heart.

✧ What Changed My Life

The moment I began choosing my feelings instead of being pulled by my emotions, I felt my own strength return. I stopped performing sadness just because I was expected to. I stopped forcing positivity when I was tired. And most importantly, I permitted myself to feel fully, without judgment. That permission changed everything.

✧ If You're Reading This

Pause when an emotion hits you. Ask: Is this really mine? Or is this what I think I'm supposed to feel? It's not weak to feel. It's not strong enough to suppress. The real strength lies in choosing what to keep and what to let go.

Strength Comes from Choosing Emotions and Feelings

Strength isn't about being emotionless—it's about being emotionally aware and intentional. In a world where reactions are automatic, true power lies in choosing how you feel and how you respond. We often think emotions just happen to us. But the truth is, after the first wave hits, we have the choice to either carry it, shift it, or let it go. Choosing emotions doesn't mean suppressing or faking them. It means being present enough to feel, reflect, and then decide what serves your growth. Anger can become boundaries. Sadness can become depth. Joy can become a way of living, not just a moment. When we realize that feelings are not facts and emotions are not commands, we begin to reclaim our power. Awareness gives us the space to choose, and that space is where emotional strength is born. Choosing your emotions doesn't make you less real—it makes you more responsible for your inner world. And that's where lasting strength lives—not in control, but in conscious response.

Chapter 2: The Choice of a Positive Approach

"Positivity isn't just a personality trait — it's a daily choice. In this chapter, I'll share how choosing awareness and action brought joy, growth, and strength into my life, even when things didn't go as planned

Exploring Inner Happiness with Awareness

Back in my 10th grade, we were given a school project in Telugu class—to create a model of a village. I still remember how deeply involved I was in that little project. I used cardboard sheets, thick paper, and whatever I could find to bring a small, vibrant village to life. I made tiny houses, added greenery, built roads—every detail filled with care. I was present, fully alive in the making of it.

I did it with so much joy in my heart, imagining how my teacher would react. I hoped for a "10 out of 10" and maybe even a sweet comment. I stored it in the classroom cupboard, proud of my little creation. But the reality? My teacher never even glanced at it. I asked, but there was no response. No words. Not even a moment of recognition.

For years, whenever I thought about that moment, I felt a sting of sadness. I believed I deserved appreciation, and it hurt that I didn't get it. But recently, when I looked back again, with a different awareness, I smiled. Not because someone finally praised it, but because I remembered the joy I felt while making it.

That project wasn't about marks. It was about presence. It was about me, sitting with glue on my fingers, excited about every tree I pasted. That joy was real, and it still lives inside me.

This is what I mean by choosing happiness through awareness.

We often tie our happiness to outcomes, to validation, to recognition. But what if the happiness was already there—in the doing, in the being, in the creating?

Today, I don't see that project as a failure to be seen. I see it as a success in feeling alive. I didn't lose anything. I gained a memory of presence and creation that still brings a smile to my face.

So, I invite you to ask:

Are you measuring joy by results, or are you honouring the joy that already exists in the process?

Happiness isn't always in what you get. Sometimes, it's in what you give, feel, and live while you're doing it.

I once read a quote that said, "Happiness is not something ready-made. It comes from your own actions." That line stayed with me. I didn't want to wait for someone else to bring joy into my life — I wanted to explore what it would feel like to create it myself.

So I began observing. Noticing.

I looked for little sparks of joy in the people around me — a kind gesture from a stranger, the way my friend laughed without holding back, the peace on someone's face when they sat in silence with a cup of coffee.

And then, I tried to find those same sparks within me.

Slowly, I started to live with more awareness. I didn't need a perfect day to smile. I began celebrating my small wins, choosing calm over chaos, and feeling deeply grateful for moments that once seemed ordinary.

Positivity wasn't something I had to borrow — that was something I could build. With intention, with softness, with presence.

And the more I explored it within myself, the more I began to see it in everyone and everything around me.

Choose to wake up with a smile every day – that hits different, experience it.

The Choice That I Made in My Love

Love is not always a two-way street. Sometimes, it's just you, holding the emotion with grace, not seeking a return, but simply choosing to love because you want to.

I once loved a man who didn't love me back. But unlike the stories where pain turns to bitterness, I didn't choose to dwell or depend emotionally. I chose to love purely.

While others might've waited for attention, I created memories. I sketched the moments we shared, not because I wanted him to notice, but because I wanted to remember what I felt. I wrote poems to pour out my heart — not to get a reply, but to give space for my truth. I texted him sometimes, knowing well I might not get an answer — but I never held that against him. I kept WhatsApp statuses, not as silent cries for attention, but as quiet declarations of the joy I found in loving him.

And here's the miracle:
That unreturned love made me more me.

I became a better writer.
I began crafting songs.
My poetry is amazing.
My positivity strengthened.

I started to create — not for him, but because love awakened something powerful within me.

It reminded me of what SP. Bala Subrahmanyam Garu once said:

“Love is the ultimate thing. You can always choose to love and explore, because love “gives”. It gives creativity. It makes you write, sing, paint, and live deeply.”

So today, years of my love journey became years of blessings — a sacred time where I didn’t just love someone...

...I discovered the kind of woman I could become by loving. And that was enough.

- Have you ever tried to find out what love lets you explore?
- What hidden part of yourself did love gently awaken?
- Can you allow love to shape you, even when it doesn’t look the way you imagined?

✨ **Remember:** Love doesn’t always need a destination. Sometimes, it just wants to move through you—and in doing so, transform you. And sometimes love doesn’t come to stay—it comes to reveal.

Suggestion: Choose to explore within love, not just seek the feeling of being loved.

[Curious to ask: did you ever sketch your movements together?

My advice to beautiful love, sketch memories even if you are bad at that, because whenever you feel sad, just watch them, you get a smile automatically.]

Part II: Choosing Love Consciously

Chapter 3: Choose to Show Love Instead of Hiding It

Love as a gift, not a fearful attachment.

Love is not just a feeling we carry inside — it's a choice we make to let others feel it too.
In this chapter, we explore the everyday ways we can express love, not through grand gestures, but through simple presence, kind words, and thoughtful actions.

Because love that stays hidden often fades.
But love that's shown, even in the smallest ways, has the power to heal, strengthen, and make life beautifully meaningful.

I used to think people would just know I cared. But over time, I've learned — unspoken love is often unheard love. So now, I choose to show it, say it, and share it.

Express Love Through Presence, Words, and Action

Love isn't just about romance. It's the quiet emotion that lives in your heart for your parents, your siblings, your friends, your mentors, even your pets. It's not something to be held back or hidden, waiting for a perfect moment or a poetic way to say it.

You don't need to be expressive or artistic to show love. You don't have to craft songs or write letters. Just a small message, a smile, a gentle hand on the shoulder — these are powerful too. Don't worry about whether it will be understood, appreciated, or returned. That's not the point.

The magic of love is in feeling it as you give it — without fear, without judgment. Whether it's a heartfelt message to a friend, cooking a meal for your parents, or sitting silently beside someone who needs you — every act becomes sacred when done with presence.

I learned this by practicing it. When I stopped overthinking and started showing my love simply and freely, I felt lighter, warmer, more human.

Sometimes, it's as simple as:

• Making your mother her favourite tea without being asked.

• Texting a friend just to say, "I thought of you today."

• Sitting with your pet and talking to them like they're your whole world.

• Gently placing your hand on someone's shoulder when words aren't enough.

None of these require a return. None of them need approval.

You don't need to wait until someone is gone to say what you wish you'd said. Love isn't something you keep hidden hoping it will be safe — it's something you share, so it grows.

Let your love be spoken, shown, and shared. Not because you want it back, but because choosing to love openly is choosing to live honestly.

Love Unspoken Is Love Wasted

I've seen people hold back love because of fear:

- Fear of judgment.
- Fear of rejection.
- Fear of seeming too emotional.

But the truth is — unspoken love doesn't protect you, it burdens you.

Say "I'm proud of you" to your sibling when they try something new.

Tell your friend, "Your presence makes my life better." Write that message, even if it feels silly. Smile with meaning. Hug with presence.

Even if they don't respond the way you hoped — your love wasn't wasted. You honoured it by expressing it. And in doing so, you freed yourself from the regret of silence

"It's better to be open-hearted than to wonder forever what might have been."

One time, I went to a family function. I was dressed up, hopeful, and surrounded by the people I call my own — my brothers, my family. Each of my brothers had an iPhone. Yet not one of them turned their camera toward me. Not one said, "Let me take a picture of you." Not one tried to make me feel seen.

I stood there, quietly, a little distant... and I saw something that stayed with me. A man — not very well-off, his phone wasn't even a good one — was busy clicking pictures of the woman beside him. Smiling at her. Making her feel beautiful. Special. Present.

That's when I felt it deeply: love that's unexpressed can feel like absence.

Maybe my brothers do love me. Maybe they feel responsible. But in that moment, I didn't feel it — and that's what matters. Because love isn't just a thought. It's a gesture. A picture. A word. A little effort.

We think people know how we feel — but they don't always. We think silence is safer — but it leaves too much unsaid.

Even the smallest action can become someone's warmest memory.

A photo. A compliment. A "you look nice today." A hand on the shoulder. A shared smile in a crowded room.

These are the little ways we say: I see you. You matter to me. So don't wait. Don't assume. Don't store your love in silence. Say it. Show it. Give it. Because unspoken love may stay in your heart, ...but it never reaches theirs.

We may not always control what happens, but we can always choose how we respond — with love, with awareness, with intention.

Chapter 4: Choosing Feelings in Love and Relationships.

Loving Someone vs. Wanting to Be Loved

Many of us go through phases in life where we feel a deep urge to be loved—especially when we're lonely, insecure, or trying to fill an emotional gap. In those moments, it's easy to believe we're loving someone, but in truth, we may just be desperately hoping to be loved back.

This confusion leads to repeated cycles of disappointment. You think you're in love, but what you're actually doing is reaching out, hoping someone will finally offer the emotional comfort you haven't given yourself. So when things don't go well—or when that person doesn't respond the way you expected—you feel unloved, abandoned, or not enough. And instead of pausing to reflect, we often move on to the next person, expecting them to fill that same void.

Over time, this pattern builds pain. You jump from one connection to another, searching for love like it's something you can find outside of yourself—when the truth is, the feeling of love begins within you. You don't find love by seeking it, you feel love by choosing it—by becoming someone who has it to give, even before it's returned.

Real love happens when you feel whole already. When you're not depending on the other person to make you feel good, wanted, or safe. You're just choosing to love, because that's who you are. It's a flow, not a need.

So if you've ever found yourself feeling empty after being in love, or disappointed again and again, pause and ask:

Was I truly loving someone—or was I hoping they would finally love me enough to fix the parts of me I hadn't healed yet?

Being Aware While Loving — Choosing Your Feelings Before Your Partner

One of the most misunderstood truths about love is this: **feelings can happen naturally, but staying committed is a conscious choice.** You might be deeply in love with someone and still feel drawn to someone else. That doesn't necessarily mean your love was fake. It means you're human, and humans are emotional beings, constantly responding to moments, energy, and people.

A kind gesture, a moment of care, an unexpected connection—it can stir emotions in us, even when we're already in a relationship. But this is where awareness matters. **If you're unaware of your emotions, you start to follow every feeling as truth**, and that's where real damage begins. You start thinking, "Maybe this new person is my real love," or "Maybe I never truly loved the first one."

But here's a truth you rarely hear:

You're not loving the new person. You're loving the way they made you feel in a particular moment.

And that moment might pass.

Awareness gives you the power to pause. It gives you the space to observe: "Okay, I'm feeling something. But why? What need is this filling? What part of me is reacting?" When you're emotionally aware, you don't let your feelings drive your decisions—you guide them. You understand that emotions are valid, but not always instructions.

And most importantly, you realize that choosing your relationship isn't about denying emotions—it's about **prioritizing what you've built with love**, trust, and effort over a temporary emotional high.

So, here's the reminder:

Your partner isn't responsible for controlling your feelings—you are.

Even if you feel something for someone else, it doesn't mean you've betrayed your love. But if you follow those feelings blindly without awareness, that's when betrayal begins.

You have to choose your feelings, process them, and decide how to act on them—not because you owe someone perfection, but because you owe yourself honesty.

Did you ever get feelings for someone even though you were already in a relationship? – Aware that you are human. feelings are common to humans; choose them.

Chapter 5: Choose to Give Love, Not Attach Emotionally

Emotional Attachment Is Fear in Disguise

There was a time I thought staying close to someone, needing their constant attention, reply, or validation, meant love. I didn't realize that what I called "love" was sometimes fear in disguise.

Fear of being alone. Fear of not being enough. Fear that if I didn't hold tightly, they'd leave.

But true love isn't about gripping. It's about giving — freely, without needing something back to feel whole.

Emotional attachment often comes from a space of insecurity — where we seek someone else to complete a part of us we haven't yet embraced ourselves. But when you start choosing love with freedom, you feel lighter. You don't love someone because they fill a gap — you love them because your heart is full enough to overflow.

I realized this especially in moments where I used to wait for a reply, feel hurt by silence, or get anxious if someone didn't react the way I wanted.

Then I asked myself: "What if I gave love because it's who I am, not because I want something back?"

That shift changed everything. I began to see the difference between:

• Loving with freedom

• And attaching out of fear

Now, coming to the choice of another perspective

(Let them choose us with no attachments.) Here you know how?

We often talk about attachment and detachment like they are the only ways to relate. But what if there's something more mature, more powerful — where you don't bind people, but instead let them feel free with you?

During my college days, I had a roommate. We weren't deeply emotionally attached or overly expressive. But one day, she looked at me and said,

"I feel so comfortable with you. I don't feel judged. I can share anything without fear or pressure."

That moment stayed with me. It made me realize: we don't need to be emotionally intense to build meaningful bonds. We just need to be emotionally safe.

So, what did I do?

Nothing big — I just let her be. I never expected her to talk, share, or behave in a certain way. I didn't over-ask or over-give. I simply stayed available and non-demanding.

And in that space, she felt free. Free to be open, free to be herself — free to choose me.

That's what love those flows look like. It's not about pulling someone closer or pushing them away. It's about being someone others can rest with, not worry about.

Many women, at various stages in their lives, find themselves struggling with emotional attachment and the fear that comes with it. Whether it's a friend, partner, or family member, the thought of becoming emotionally dependent or "maintaining" someone else's emotional well-being can feel overwhelming. We often find ourselves tangled in relationships where we fear stepping back, worrying that the other person might become disturbed or even lost without us. This attachment can leave us feeling trapped, as if we're the ones holding up the emotional foundation of the relationship. But the truth is, emotional attachment doesn't have to define our relationships or our sense of self-worth. It's a pattern we can choose to break, and in doing so, we not only free ourselves but also allow the other person the space to grow and manage their own emotions. Here's a process you can follow to create healthier emotional connections without feeling burdened.

How to Create a Balanced Space Without Feeling Like You're "Maintaining"

1. Set Boundaries with Compassion

You're not abandoning your friend, but you can choose to set clear boundaries that protect your emotional space. The key here is to communicate those boundaries with kindness, making it clear that you care but you also need balance in your life.

For example:

"I really care about you, and I enjoy our conversations, but I also need time for myself to recharge. Both of us need to be able to have space and not feel dependent on each other for constant attention." This shows you care, but also makes it clear that you're not always available to engage in emotional conversations. This way, your friend knows it's not a personal rejection, but a necessity for your well-being.

2. Encourage Their Independence

Your friend may have become emotionally dependent on you, but by showing them it's okay to handle things on their own, you can encourage emotional growth. Encourage them to explore other support systems, like other friends or even professional help.

For example, you can say:

"I'm glad you're talking to me, but have you thought about talking to a counsellor or a group of friends for a wider perspective? I think it would be great for you to have multiple people to lean on, not just me." This creates space for both of you to have the freedom to grow without feeling burdened.

3. Shift the Dynamic to Mutual Growth

Instead of feeling like you're maintaining them, encourage your friend to shift focus from always seeking emotional support to also offering support. This gives the relationship a more balanced dynamic. You might say: "I love when we can talk, but I also love when we can share things that make us grow. How about we share some things we're learning or trying out instead of just talking about our struggles?" This helps focus on shared growth and deepens the connection without the need for constant emotional "maintenance."

4. Trust That They Can Handle Your Absence

This is often the hardest part — trusting that your friend can be okay without constant interaction. People grow through independence, and as much as we want to care for them, sometimes stepping back and giving space allows them to build resilience. If you stop being available all the time, your friend will adapt and might even discover new ways of coping. It's crucial to trust that they will be okay.

5. Focus on Emotional Health for Both

If you feel guilty about taking space, remember: your emotional health matters too. If you're drained, you're not able to show up as the friend they deserve. Focus on activities that restore you — whether it's journaling, reading, exercise, or meditating — and model this behavior to your friend. Encourage them to take care of their own mental health as well.

For example:

"I've been finding that when I focus on taking care of myself, I feel so much better. Maybe we could try doing something that helps us both, like going for a walk or reading something uplifting?"

Final Thoughts: You're not abandoning your friend by setting boundaries or making space for yourself. You're simply choosing to make the relationship healthier for both of you. This is a form of self-respect and kindness, not just to yourself but to them as well. By showing them that they can manage their emotions without relying on you all the time, you're actually teaching them a very valuable lesson: that their well-being doesn't have to depend on another person's constant presence.

True Love Expects Nothing—It Flows

Love is never a transaction; it's a flowing exchange where both people have the power to choose how they give and receive. It's not about what you expect from the other person; it's about freely offering yourself without attaching conditions.

I recall a time when I made a dish for my love, poured all my energy and care into it, hoping it would be something special. But to my surprise, he didn't enjoy that kind of food. I was faced with two options: I could hold on to my ego, refuse to change, and feel hurt that my efforts weren't recognized, or I could choose to set my pride aside and make something he would appreciate.

On one hand, I could stick to my choice, making something I believed showed love. But on the other hand, I realized that love isn't just about what I feel; it's also about understanding the other person. By choosing to let go of my ego and prepare something he would enjoy, I was showing love in a way that truly made us both happy.

This moment made me realize that love is about choosing what's best for both people, even when it means letting go of your own expectations. It's not about forcing someone to love you the way you want them to. It's about letting go of your ego to create space where both people can feel loved, respected, and happy.

In relationships, we often have options on both sides—our pride or our connection. If I choose to let go of my ego and make something he loves, and he chooses to let go of his ego and enjoy what I lovingly prepared, we both create a space where love flows freely. True love isn't shown only in grand gestures but also in the small, quiet choices we make to meet each other with softness, understanding, and respect. Instead of thinking they have to recognize your efforts, put your efforts just because you love. That makes your emotions clear and creates peace in your heart.

Not all efforts will be shown by making something for someone. Sometimes, some efforts will also hide in letting your ego down.

Chapter 6: Choose to Live, Not Just Dream

Don't Wait for the Right Time—Start Now

I used to think there was a "right time" for everything. The perfect moment to start writing, the ideal conditions to begin a project, the most supportive environment to follow my dreams. I waited. I doubted. I hesitated.

But the truth is, waiting for perfection is the most beautiful way to postpone life. We imagine a t ime where everything aligns—but life rarely offers that. What it gives instead is the present moment, full of quiet possibilities, wrapped in a little fear and a little hope.

I learned that dreams don't start in perfect conditions. They start when we decide to live them. I didn't know the outcome of what I was creating—this book, my writing, or even my expressions of love. But I chose to begin. That beginning became my teacher. That imperfect step forward turned into confidence.

You don't need to be ready. You just need to begin. You don't need to be fearless. You just need to be honest. You don't need all the answers. You just need the courage to ask the first question.

Waiting delays your becoming. Starting welcomes your becoming.

So I ask you gently:

What are you dreaming of? And what if today is already the "right time" you were waiting for?

Start, even if your hands shake. Start, even if your voice trembles. Because living begins not when the world says yes… …but when you stop saying no to yourself.

WHEN I STARTED LIVING IN DREAM

I remember when I was in my final year, my friend Ajay and I decided to start a business together. We didn't have everything figured out. We didn't even know where or how to begin. But we had a dream—and more importantly, we chose to explore it.

That choice took me to Hyderabad for the first time. I still remember the excitement running through my body like it was electricity. I met a big businessman and gathered the courage to talk to him—just talking to someone like that felt like an achievement. It was a proud moment I'll never forget.

Later, we tried to market eco-friendly covers in Rajahmundry. We didn't know how the journey would go—we just kept walking forward. One shopkeeper connected us to a nearby vendor in Nidadavole. So we decided, why not? Let's go.

We stepped into that village together. For me, it was the first time seeing a village like that—and the beauty of it touched something in me. It wasn't about whether we'd succeed. It wasn't about profit or plans. It was about the feel of living our dream in motion. That six-month journey was filled with learning, laughter, mistakes, growth, and deep presence.

We didn't wait for the "right time." We made time right by stepping in.

Sometimes dreams don't need a destination. They just need direction.

You don't always need clarity. You need curiosity. And even if the dream shifts or changes or fails—what you gain by choosing to live it is always worth it.

So if there's a little dream knocking on your heart, I hope this reminds you: You don't need a plan. You need a pulse.

Dreams Need Action, Not Perfection.

We spend too much time trying to get it all "right." The right moment. The right plan. The right skills. The perfect timing. But dreams don't ask for perfect. They ask for presence.

Waiting for perfection is like waiting at a bus stop for a train. You'll keep missing what was meant for you—just because it didn't arrive in the form you expected.

I've realized something on my journey: The boldest step you'll ever take is not doing something perfectly. It's doing it while you're unsure, scared, unprepared—and still showing up.

You don't write your first poem because it's perfect. You write because your heart has something to say. You don't start a business because you know it will succeed. You start because the dream inside you matters more than the fear around you. You don't become a creator because someone approved of you. You become one because you chose to begin.

Your dream doesn't need your confidence. It needs your commitment.

Don't wait to become fearless. Don't wait to become flawless. Don't wait to become fully ready. Just begin. Be a little messy. Let the journey teach you.

Because perfection is an illusion, but action is a decision.

What if you have no one to support, don't blame, just choose you

Before we ever explored business seriously, I always had a quiet dream in my heart—to start my own e-commerce store.

But honestly, I made it feel harder than it was. I thought I needed GST numbers, government licenses, and a perfect setup. I overwhelmed myself with assumptions and never even gave it a try.

People might say, "**You had a supportive friend**, so it's easier for you."

But here's a truth many don't realize:

Every person has their own responsibilities, dreams, and directions. After our graduation, my friend Ajay started looking for a job—and I knew that was his journey. Mine was different. I didn't want to do a job. I wanted to explore what e-commerce actually was.

So, I took the step alone.

I explored platforms like Meesho. And guess what? It was so much simpler than I imagined. I learned how to upload products, handle orders, respond to customers, and track shipping. Things I thought were complicated became clearer only after I tried.

If I had started in college, just by choosing to explore, maybe we would have grown bigger already. But still—I'm glad I began when I did.

And that's what I want to tell you.

When you carry a dream like a seed in your heart—don't wait for someone to water it.

Choose to water it yourself.
Choose to learn.
Choose to search.
Choose to begin.

Don't wait until you feel "ready" for the result.

Prepare yourself to start.
Let yourself explore.
Let your dream live.

Even if the outcome is uncertain, the journey will always teach you something your imagination never could.

Choose Peace in the Process

I'm not here to say I became a successful businesswoman overnight.

No, I didn't build an empire — not yet. But I did something more important: **I chose to step in.**

Because success doesn't always arrive with applause and big results. Sometimes, it begins quietly — the moment you choose to move forward, despite uncertainty.

Many people hold on to the belief: "If I work hard, one day success will come."

And yes — effort matters. But so does peace of mind while working. Because if we only chase results, we miss the beauty of the process. And when results delay or don't come the way we imagined, we end up frustrated, disappointed, or worse — we stop believing.

But what if we flipped that belief?

What if we choose to celebrate the small wins — the courage to start, the lessons learned, the growth felt?

What if we choose peace over pressure? What if we realize that positivity doesn't have to be attracted — it's already within us when we work from joy, not fear?

I may not be "there" yet. But I've started.

I'm learning.

I'm growing.

And in that, I'm already successful.

Because success isn't just about what you reach — It's about how you choose to walk the path.

Mindfulness Exercise: "Before reacting to any situation, take a deep breath. Inhale for four counts, hold for four counts, and exhale for four counts. In this pause, observe your feelings, thoughts, and physical sensations without judgment. Ask yourself: 'What is my true choice here?'"

Takeaway: Don't wait for the perfect moment — create it. Choose action over assumption. Choose to explore rather than expect. And most importantly, choose peace in the process, not pressure from the result. Because when you step in with love for your dream, every moment becomes a win.

Part III: Choose Awareness Over Appearance

Part III: Choose Awareness Over Appearance

Being good is often about fitting in. Being real is about showing up. In a world where it's easy to hide behind masks, we often forget that true strength lies in being real. In this part, we dive into the importance of choosing self-awareness over creating an image — not just for others, but for ourselves. Because when we are aware, we stop performing and start living authentically. It's about knowing who we are, beyond the surface, and embracing the courage to show up as we truly are.

Chapter 7: Don't Wear the Mask of Goodness

So often, we find ourselves caught in the act of being "good" — not because we genuinely want to be, but because it's expected of us. In this chapter, we explore how pretending to be good can hinder our true growth. It's about shedding the mask of perfection and choosing authenticity over approval. Being real requires courage, and sometimes, it's harder to show up as our true selves than to play the part. But true goodness, the one that comes from within, is far more liberating.

We Pretend to Be Good Instead of Honest

In this section, I explore the tendency many of us have to mask our true selves under the guise of "goodness." Whether it's a desire to fit in, to avoid conflict, or to gain approval, we often sacrifice honesty for the sake of appearing virtuous. The pressure to be "good" can be so overwhelming that we end up suppressing our real feelings, desires, and beliefs.

I recall moments in my life when I prioritized being perceived as good over being true to myself. For example, there were times when I agreed to things I didn't feel aligned with just to please others. I smiled through situations that made me uncomfortable, simply because I believed that being polite and accommodating was the "right" thing to do. In the process, I was not being honest with myself or with others. Instead of honouring my true feelings and opinions, I wore a mask of goodness to avoid judgment or rejection.

But the more I did this, the more I felt disconnected from myself. I realized that the mask I wore was not just hiding my true self — it was creating a version of me that I no longer recognized or felt comfortable with. In trying to appear good, I lost touch with what truly mattered to me. And the more I kept pretending, the more I felt like I was living a life that wasn't entirely mine.

This chapter encourages us to step away from that mask. It's about realizing that true goodness comes from honesty, even if it means being vulnerable or imperfect. When we start being honest, we let go of the burden of pretence and allow ourselves to connect with others on a deeper level. Authenticity, not perfection, is the key to real goodness. When we let go of the need to appear good, we create space to simply be ourselves, and that is where true fulfilment lies.

Choosing honesty over pretence is liberating. It allows us to live with integrity, to make decisions that align with our values, and to have relationships that are genuine, rather than based on false expectations. So, in this section, we'll explore how to recognize when we're pretending to be good and how to make the conscious choice to replace the mask with authenticity.

Here's a list of regular daily habits where we often wear masks, pretending to be "good" instead of being honest with ourselves:

1. **Agreeing to Work Tasks Outside Your Responsibility:** Accepting extra work from your boss or colleagues just to

avoid conflict or appear cooperative, even when it's not in your job description or beyond your capacity.

2. **Saying "Yes" to Social Invitations Even When You're Tired:** Agreeing to go out with friends, even when you're exhausted or would prefer some alone time, simply to avoid disappointing them.

3. **Offering Food or Resources When You Can't Afford It:** Sharing or offering food or resources to others when you're running low, simply to appear generous, even though you're struggling yourself.

4. **Pretending to Enjoy Something You Don't Like**: Agreeing with others or pretending to enjoy an activity, hobby, or conversation that you don't care about, just to avoid being judged or alienating others.

5**. Staying Silent in Uncomfortable Situations:** Keeping quiet in situations where you feel uncomfortable or even wronged, out of fear of confrontation or upsetting others.

6. **Tolerating Disrespectful Behaviour:** Accepting disrespect or inappropriate behaviour from others because you're afraid of addressing it, thinking it's better to remain "polite" than confront the issue.

7. **Overcommitting Yourself to Help Others**: Taking on too many commitments for friends or family out of a sense of obligation, even when it stretches your time and energy beyond what you can manage.

8. **Suppressing Your True Feelings in Relationships**: Hiding your emotions or pretending everything is okay when it's not, just to keep the peace in relationships — whether romantic, familial, or friendly.

9. **Faking a Smile or Positive Attitude at Work**: Putting on a cheerful face or pretending to be motivated at work, even if you're feeling drained or unhappy, because you believe it's expected of you.

10. **Saying "I'm Fine" When You're Not:** Responding with "I'm fine" when you're clearly not, simply to avoid burdening others or making them worry, even though expressing your true feelings would be healthier for both you and them.

These are just a few examples of the many ways we wear masks in our daily lives, often out of a desire to avoid conflict, disappointment, or judgment. But these actions, over time, can disconnect us from our true selves, leading to frustration and inner conflict. Recognizing these moments and choosing authenticity, rather than performing goodness, is the first step toward living a more fulfilling and true-to-yourself life.

I want to share a moment that truly changed my understanding of this.

There was a time when my dad needed urgent medicine. A friend of mine offered to help bring it. I trusted him and waited. But the next day, he didn't answer my calls. He avoided me—not with cruelty, but with silence. I could sense that he still wanted to be seen as a good person, someone who cares, someone reliable. Maybe he thought circumstances came in the way. Maybe he thought not helping would disappoint me or make me see him differently.

But here's the truth: **if he had told me honestly that he couldn't bring the medicine, I would have respected him more**. I would have quickly asked someone else, and things would have moved on without any disappointment. What hurt more than his "no" was the silence. The pretending. The fear of being honest.

This moment taught me something powerful: **don't wear the mask of goodness.** If you can't help, say it. If you don't have space, communicate it. True value in relationships comes from clarity, not performance. Pretending to be available when you're not doesn't make you good; it just makes things harder for both sides.

We think people will stop respecting us if we say "no." But **respect grows when honesty shows**. I wasn't expecting miracles. I was only expecting the truth.

Let's choose this kind of honesty. Let's give others the chance to make different choices when we can't show up. And let's free ourselves from the fear of not being liked by choosing integrity over image.

Choose Awareness Over Image

Choose Awareness Over the Image We Carry in Society

We live in a world where so much attention is given to "what others think of me." From the way we speak, dress, post on social media, or even express emotions, many of our actions are unconsciously driven by how we're perceived. But what about how we perceive ourselves?

The image we carry for society is often carefully built—layered with politeness, perfection, achievements, smiles, and silent compromises. But deep inside, if we are not aware of who we really are and how we really feel, that image becomes a burden.

Awareness is freedom. It's not loud. It doesn't seek attention. It quietly asks:

- Do I really want this?
- Am I doing this for validation?
- Is this version of me true?

For example:

• You may wear clothes you don't like just to match expectations.

• You may say you're “doing fine” when you're actually struggling.

• You may act confident, while your inner voice craves support.

But the truth is: **peace doesn’t come from managing your image; it comes from understanding your inner world.**

When you begin to choose awareness over appearance, you:

• Feel lighter.

• Express more honestly.

• Build genuine relationships.

• Stop chasing approval.

The image will fade, but awareness will stay. It is your awareness that lets you evolve—not the applause you receive outside. So, next time you find yourself adjusting to fit in—pause and ask, "Is this me, or the image I carry?"

Real Goodness vs. Performed Goodness

In today’s world, many people confuse being good with appearing good. But there's a quiet difference—one that shapes the foundation of trust, respect, and meaningful relationships.

Real goodness comes from sincerity. It doesn’t seek praise. It doesn’t act out of fear. It does what is possible—and speaks honestly about what isn’t.

Performed goodness, on the other hand, is like wearing a smile that hides discomfort. It:

• Overpromises and underdelivers.

• Says “yes” just to avoid guilt or judgment.

• Cares more about being seen as kind than being truly honest.

Let me share a real-life experience.

I had a friend who offered to bring medicine for my father. I didn’t ask—he offered. I felt relieved and trusted his word. But the next day, he didn’t answer my calls. He didn’t deliver the medicine. And he didn’t even explain why. Maybe he had genuine reasons. Maybe life got in the way. But instead of gently telling me, “I’m sorry, I can’t,” he avoided me altogether.

And that changed everything.

Because here's the truth: If he had simply refused, respectfully and clearly, I would have still respected him. I could've made another arrangement. But when someone tries to appear good instead of being honest, it leaves behind confusion, hurt, and mistrust.

Goodness isn't about saying yes—it's about meaning what you say

Let's normalize:

• Gently refusing when we can't help.

• Being upfront about our limits.

• Letting others know they matter, even when we can't show up for them.

Real goodness is rooted in clarity, not performance. It doesn't wear a mask. It doesn't fear rejection. It shows up with presence, or speaks with truth when it cannot.

Choose to Be the Real You

Choosing to be real is not just an act of courage—it's an act of deep self-respect.

When you choose to be honest over impressive, clear over confusing, and genuine over accepted, you build a life rooted in truth. And that life attracts the right people—those who value who you are, not the image you wear.

You don't have to agree to everything to be seen as kind. You don't have to carry others' expectations to prove your worth. You don't have to perform. You just have to show up as you—with boundaries, honesty, and care.

Even in small moments—like saying "I can't help right now" or "I'm not comfortable with this"— you're planting seeds of real trust.

Because the real you is enough.

In a world full of masks, **being real is rare**—and deeply powerful.

So, choose to be real, even when it's uncomfortable. That's where true goodness begins.

Chapter 8: The Mirror of Self-Deception

Sometimes, the hardest truths aren't the ones we hide from the world—they're the ones we hide from ourselves. We convince ourselves we've moved on when we haven't. We act strong while silently breaking. We tell ourselves we're fine just to avoid facing the fear, pain, or insecurity that lingers underneath. This chapter isn't about judging those deceptions. It's about gently recognizing them. Because true growth begins when we stop performing for our own reflection and start meeting ourselves as we are—with honesty, curiosity, and courage. This is not about blaming—it's about awakening. And awareness is the first act of self-love.

Many People Aren't Lying to Others—They're Unconsciously Lying to Themselves

We often imagine lies as something we tell others. But some of the most powerful and persistent lies are the ones we quietly whisper to ourselves, without even realizing it.

We say we're over someone when deep down, a message from them can still shake us. We say we've healed when we've only buried the pain under distraction. We call our fear "logic," our guilt "kindness," our avoidance "peace."

These aren't intentional lies—they're emotional survival mechanisms. They help us cope. They help us function. But they also hold us back.

You can't grow past a truth you haven't faced. You can't become who you truly are if you're still wearing layers of stories that aren't real.

This doesn't mean you've failed—it means you're human. And the first step toward becoming honest with the world is learning how to be deeply, quietly honest with yourself.

ASK:

• Am I pretending I don't care just to protect myself?

• Am I staying busy to avoid something uncomfortable inside me?

• Am I afraid of who I'll find if I stop performing strength?

You don't need to answer all at once. You only need to be willing to ask. Because self-deception isn't weakness—it's a call to meet yourself more gently, more bravely, and more truly.

Takeaway: We often say "I'm okay" when we're not. Not to fool others—but because we're afraid of what honesty will uncover. Growth begins the moment we stop hiding from our own hearts.

Psychological Growth Requires Seeing Your Shadows, Not Just Your Strengths

Ravi is known for being the "calm one" in every group. He prides himself on never yelling, never arguing, always keeping peace. Everyone admires his patience.

But when something bothers him deeply—he shuts down, disappears, or silently holds resentment. He never shares what he feels because he thinks anger is "ugly" and "not spiritual."

What's the shadow here?

Ravi's strength is his calmness. But his shadow is suppressed anger. He avoids conflict at all costs—not because he's evolved, but because he's afraid of emotional mess. His silence isn't peace—it's fear dressed as peace.

He can't grow until he accepts that even his anger is valid, and being calm doesn't mean hiding what hurts

We live in a world that constantly asks us to show our best — our achievements, talents, and strengths. We're encouraged to shine, to stand out, to "be positive." But real growth doesn't come from only highlighting what's good in us. It also comes from facing what's hidden — our shadows.

Shadows are the parts of us we often ignore, deny, or feel ashamed of. Our anger. Our jealousy. Our fear of not being enough. Our need for validation. These aren't weaknesses — they are truths. And until we face them, they quietly control our choices.

You may be kind, but are you kind just to be liked? You may be responsible, but do you carry resentment because you never say no? You may appear confident, but are you constantly comparing yourself in silence?

True psychological growth starts when we stop editing ourselves to appear perfect and begin meeting ourselves with honesty. Growth is not about "fixing" who we are. It's about understanding who we are — completely.

It's uncomfortable. It may even hurt. But it's also freeing.

Because when you see your shadow clearly, it no longer has power over you.

Awareness Means Having the Courage to Meet Your Real Self, Even When It's Uncomfortable

Awareness isn't just about knowing what's right or wrong — it's about noticing what we actually do, what we feel, and how we respond in real-time. Most people think self-awareness is a soft, gentle word. But in truth, it's one of the most uncomfortable and courageous things a person can choose.

It's uncomfortable to admit when we're being passive-aggressive. It's uncomfortable to notice we're trying to please others while pretending we're confident. It's uncomfortable to realize that we're repeating the same unhealthy pattern again.

But the moment we begin to observe our behaviour instead of just reacting... we open the door to change.

- Did I say "yes" when I wanted to say "no"?
- Did I blame someone else when I was the one feeling insecure?
- Did I scroll through my phone because I was avoiding a tough conversation?

These little reflections become turning points. They're not judgments. They're opportunities. Opportunities to choose better. To respond consciously. To grow.

Awareness is not perfection. It's progress.

And it begins when you stop lying to yourself that everything is fine, and gently ask, "Why did I act that way?"

That's the moment you meet your real self — not the image, not the mask, but the you that wants to do better.

I won't change

I've observed something often — especially among teenage boys or young men in love. Many of them deeply love someone, sometimes with all their heart. But still, they carry this silent rule in their mind: "**I won't change for anyone**."

Not because they don't care. Not because their love is shallow. But because somewhere, they've been told that changing for love is a weakness. That if they admit they're affected or emotional, they're somehow less of a man.

They hold tight to ego, to an image of being "strong," "unbothered," or "independent." They fear that softening, evolving, or showing vulnerability will make them look cheap, weak, or too available.

So even when love or family knocks on their door — they don't open.

Not because they don't want to — but because they're scared that becoming better for someone else makes them "less" in the eyes of the world.

But the truth is — Real strength is not in refusing to change. It's in choosing to grow. Changing yourself for love, for family, for inner peace — isn't a sign of weakness. It's a sign of maturity. It's not about bending to others. It's about recognizing that if love is worth it, we're worth improving for.

And this awareness — noticing where your ego is louder than your love — is one of the biggest acts of self-respect you can make.

Because at the end of the day, you're not just choosing another person. You're choosing the version of you who can truly love, live, and evolve without fear.

There was a boy I once knew in college. He had a girl in his life — someone who genuinely cared for him, supported his dreams, and stood by him through his rough patches. She never demanded anything big. All she ever wanted was for him to open up a little, be more expressive, maybe show up on time, message her when he was late — simple things.

But he wouldn't. Not because he didn't love her. He did. Deeply. But he'd say things like, "This is who I am." "I don't believe in changing for anyone." "She'll understand if she really loves me."

Eventually, she stopped asking. She quietly left. And he? He didn't chase her. Not out of pride — but because he didn't know how. Years later, he admitted to a friend, "She was the only one who made me feel seen. But I was too proud to let her see the real me."

That's what happens when ego becomes our mask. When we confuse stillness with strength. When we believe that to remain the same is nobler than to grow.

So, if you ever find yourself holding back from becoming a better version of you — not because you can't, but because you think you shouldn't — pause.

Ask yourself: What's really stopping me? Fear? Pride? Or just the image I carry in front of others? Because psychological growth isn't just about celebrating who you are — it's also about humbling yourself to see what you're not yet. And in that, love finds room to breathe, evolve, and last.

Not only do relationships between men and women have ego in friendship. They sat if others and talked, then only they would. What kind of shit it is?

If you have value in someone, if you wish to talk to them, then talk. See, people are all grown up. Maybe the friendship stays with you, not the friend; they have their own responsibilities and dreams in their own life. We have to be mature enough to choose values for them. and that does mean keep a distance from them. Respect their timings.

Real strength is not in staying the same, but in choosing to grow. If love, connection, or peace asks you to reflect and shift — don't see it as losing yourself. See it as finding the version of you that's brave enough to evolve.

Part IV: Being Emotional and Bold — Both Are Choices

Part IV: Being Emotional and Bold — Both Are Choices

Choosing wisely leads to mental strength. Sometimes we believe we must either be emotional or bold, soft or strong. But real growth comes when we understand: we can be both. This part of the journey invites you to stop suppressing emotions for the sake of appearing tough, and stop avoiding strength for the fear of being "too much." When you choose with awareness, emotional depth, and bold courage can walk hand in hand — that's where true mental strength begins.

Chapter 9: The False Boldness We Wear

In a world that praises toughness, many of us learn to hide our emotional truths behind forced confidence — we speak loudly to cover our pain, we act like we don't care to avoid feeling rejected, and we push people away just to feel in control.

This chapter explores the difference between true boldness and the false bravery we often wear to survive. True boldness isn't about suppressing emotions — it's about facing them. It's about saying, "This is how I feel, and I still choose to show up."

We all want to look strong. Strong enough to not cry, strong enough to not need, strong enough to walk away without trembling.

But let's be honest: how many times have we pretended we're okay when we're not? How many times have we smiled while something inside us begged to be held, heard, or healed?

That's not real strength. That's survival-mode boldness — a mask we wear so that no one sees our soft spots.

Especially in love and close friendships, this false strength can ruin genuine connection. You say, "I don't need anyone," but the truth is you're craving someone who stays. You push people away when all you want is to be pulled closer.

The boldest thing you can do isn't shutting down. It's staying open. It's saying, "Yes, I feel deeply. Yes, I care. Yes, I'm scared — but I'm still here."

True boldness means being real, not perfect. It's choosing courage over performance. It's expressing love, asking for help, apologizing when needed, forgiving with grace — all of which require far more bravery than pretending not to feel.

Many People Think Being Emotionally Quiet = Being Mature

In today's world, silence is often mistaken for maturity. If you don't react, you're "wise." If you don't cry, you're "strong." If you don't express emotions, people assume you've grown up.

But let's pause and ask — is silence always a sign of strength? Or is it sometimes fear hiding behind a quiet face?

Many of us grew up believing that expressing pain, frustration, or sadness is "weak" or "immature." So, we shut down. We learn to suppress instead of speak. Smile instead of saying. Detach instead of deal.

But emotional silence is not always emotional strength.

True maturity isn't in holding back everything — It's in knowing when and how to express ourselves, and having the courage to do it without fear of judgment

You can sit quietly in pain, Or you can speak calmly in truth. Both take strength, but only one leads to connection and clarity.

Real maturity is not pretending to be okay. It's being aware of your feelings, accepting them, and expressing them with grace — not for attention, but for growth.

So let's stop glorifying emotional silence and start honouring emotional honesty. Because choosing to feel, express, and still carry yourself with dignity — that's not weakness. That's power in its most human form.

I still remember a moment from my diploma days.

One of my close friends, in the middle of a crowded public place, ran toward me and hugged me tightly. She was emotional, maybe overwhelmed, and she didn't hesitate to express it. But I froze.

I felt deeply uncomfortable. Not because I didn't care for her — I did — but because I wasn't used to emotions being seen. I remember thinking, "Why is she being so emotional in public?" And silently, I decided — I won't ever be like that.

I mistook her openness for weakness.

Years passed.

And in my graduation days, storms came. Life hit me with situations where I, too, wanted to break down. I needed to cry. I needed to talk. But I had trained myself to wear this invisible badge called boldness. I thought showing emotions would make me look small, soft, or immature.

But one day, when everything was too much to carry inside, I chose differently. I allowed myself to feel. I allowed myself to cry — not in helplessness, but in honesty. And for the first time, I realized something powerful:

Even pain has its moment to be respected. Even tears can be a part of a celebration — of strength, of being real, of being human.

Since then, boldness stopped being a burden. It became a choice, not a costume.

Now, if I want to cry, I cry. If I want to say "I love you," I say it. If I want to break down in someone's arms, I don't shame myself for it.

Because emotional expression is not a weakness — it's a strength that only the truly brave carry.

So, if you're still thinking maturity is about emotional silence, Let me tell you this —

True boldness is not in hiding your feelings... It's in standing beside them and still walking forward, with your heart wide open.

"Boldness is not about hiding your tears. It's about owning them. Strength isn't in silence — it's in showing up as you are, even when your voice shakes."

Avoiding My Own Heart Wasn't Courage

For a long time, I thought staying silent about my feelings made me mature. I believed that hiding my emotions was the bold thing to do, like I was protecting myself from breaking or appearing weak. But deep down, I was avoiding my own heart.

There were moments I truly wanted to reach out, to say I care, to cry, to admit I was not okay — but I swallowed all of it. I convinced myself that being unaffected was a strength. Not reacting was power. But now I know that wasn't boldness. It was fear disguised as maturity.

True courage, I've learned, is sitting with what you feel without running from it. It's choosing to be honest with yourself even when it's uncomfortable. It's saying "I miss you," or "I love you," or "I'm hurt" — not because it makes you weak, but because it makes you real.

There were times I avoided love, avoided speaking up, avoided softness — not because I didn't feel them, but because I was scared to look vulnerable. I was scared of being misunderstood, or worse, rejected. But in avoiding those emotions, I also avoided the truth of who I was.

I no longer want to be someone who avoids my heart to appear strong. I want to be someone who listens to it and lives with it — fully, honestly, and freely. That, to me, is the boldness I choose now.

You Don't Need to Be Bold. You Need to Be Honest with Yourself

For a long time, I misunderstood what boldness really meant. I thought being bold meant speaking louder, showing strength in every situation, never backing down, and carrying a constant shield around my emotions. I thought boldness was about proving myself to others — being unshakable, being right, being impressive.

But life has its own way of humbling you. I began to see that it wasn't boldness I truly needed — it was honesty. The kind of honesty that doesn't need to be shown to the world, but faced within myself. The kind that says, "Yes, I'm afraid," or "I'm not okay right now," or "This isn't who I want to become."

I've come to realize that being bold without self-honesty is just performance. It's wearing a mask to convince others — and sometimes even myself — that I've figured it all out. But when the lights go off and I'm alone, that mask feels heavy. That performance feels empty.

Real transformation began when I paused and asked myself: What do I truly feel? What do I truly want? What am I running from? And then, I sat with those answers, without judgment. That's when I started becoming not louder, but clearer. Not stronger in appearance, but deeper in understanding.

You don't have to be bold all the time. You don't have to push yourself to act like you're okay when you're not. You just need to be honest with yourself — that is where true courage begins. Boldness might impress the world, but honesty will heal your soul.

Chapter 10: The Choice of Pain

Postponed pain becomes personality. But felt pain becomes wisdom.

Pain is not just something we experience — it's something we respond to. Some people ignore it, hide it, or bury it deep, thinking that time will erase it. But in truth, pain that's not faced never really leaves — it silently shapes our personality, our beliefs, and even how we treat others. On the other hand, when we choose to feel it, to sit with it, and understand it, pain transforms. It becomes insight. It becomes depth. It becomes a strength. This chapter explores how choosing to feel our pain—instead of escaping it—is one of the most powerful choices we can ever make.

The Illusion of Fake Pain

Fake pain is the kind we often convince ourselves we're experiencing to avoid facing deeper, more uncomfortable emotions. It's the pain we attribute to external circumstances or others, but in reality, it's a shield we put up to protect ourselves from confronting the truth within. Whether it's the pain of holding onto past mistakes, staying in toxic situations, or avoiding change, fake pain keeps us in a loop of self-deception.

I've come to realize that fake pain is easy to hold onto because it allows us to avoid responsibility and growth. It's tempting to blame others for our struggles or convince ourselves that the pain is a result of something outside of us. But the more we do this, the more we stay stuck in a cycle of frustration, resentment, and self-pity.

True healing comes when we stop pretending and start acknowledging that much of the pain we carry is rooted in our own choices. Choosing to break free from fake pain means we stop hiding behind excuses and start facing the real emotions that lie beneath.

When I think back to moments in my life where I felt stuck, I can now see that I wasn't truly in pain — I was just unwilling to confront the discomfort of change. The real work begins when we embrace the discomfort and choose to grow through it.

The Conflict Between Society's Expectations and Inner Reality

Sometimes, life throws challenge our way, and we may not react the way others expect us to. For example, when something difficult happens, like a loss or a tough situation, people often expect us to feel a certain way — sad, angry, or even devastated. But the truth is, sometimes we don't feel that way at all. We might feel calm or neutral, even if everyone around us is showing strong emotions.

This can leave us feeling confused or unsure about ourselves. We might start to think, "Why am I not reacting like others? Is something wrong with me?" It's easy to believe that if we don't show emotions the "right" way, we might be seen as uncaring or distant. Society often has these unspoken rules about how we should feel in certain situations, and it can be hard not to compare ourselves to them.

But the reality is that everyone processes things differently. Just because we don't cry or show emotion in a specific way doesn't mean we're heartless. It might just mean we handle things in our own way. Some people might need more time to process, while others might have learned to keep things inside. There's no one right way to react, and it's important to understand that your own response is valid, even if it's different from what others expect.

Instead of getting caught up in how society thinks we should feel, it's better to focus on what's real for us. If we don't feel bad about something, that's okay. It doesn't mean we're ignoring the situation; it just means we're handling it in our own way. The key is to not let society's expectations make us feel like we have to force an emotion or reaction that doesn't fit.

At the end of the day, it's about accepting that your feelings are yours, and they don't have to fit into a box. If you're calm in a tough situation, that's your reality, and it's okay. Focus on what you can do to make things better, rather than trying to meet the emotional expectations of others. You can choose to process things in a way that feels right for you, and that's what matters most.

Self-Deception Through "Should" Emotions

We all have that voice in our heads telling us how things should be. It's the voice that says, "You should be stronger," or "You should be happy in this situation," or "You should feel a certain way because that's what others expect of you." For a long time, I let that voice dictate how I felt. But then I realized something crucial: those "should" weren't helping me — they were hurting me. They were convincing me to suppress how I truly felt and forcing me to follow a script that didn't fit my reality.

This kind of emotional self-deception can be subtle. You might tell yourself, "I should feel more grateful," or "I should be over this by now." You start ignoring your true feelings in the name of some ideal emotion that society, or even yourself, thinks you should have. But when you keep pushing your feelings aside, you end up ignoring the truth of your experience, and that only leads to confusion, frustration, and emotional burnout.

I've caught myself many times trying to live up to these "should" — particularly when I thought I needed to be happy or calm in a situation that was painful. But it took a lot of personal growth to realize: I didn't need to force myself to feel a certain way because of a "should." I needed to let myself feel what I was truly feeling and explore why I felt that way. Once I stopped pretending to be what I thought I should be, I started to embrace the raw, honest emotions that were coming up.

It's okay to feel sadness, anger, frustration, and confusion. Those feelings are real, and they don't need to fit into some neat little box of how we "should" feel. When I allowed myself to experience those emotions, I found that I could let go of the need to appear perfect or always in control. And that made me more authentic, not just with others, but with myself.

By breaking free from these self-imposed "shoulds," I started to realize the importance of accepting my emotions, whether they fit the ideal narrative or not. When I did, my emotional well-being improved. And the most powerful realization was that embracing my emotions, even the uncomfortable ones, brought me closer to the truth about myself.

So, stop pretending to feel how you think you should feel. Let go of the pressure to live up to others' expectations or your own fabricated standards. Choose to honour the way you truly feel, even if it's not what you think is "acceptable" or "ideal." Only then can you begin to live authentically and embrace the full spectrum of your emotions.

Self-Reflection: "Take a moment to reflect on a painful situation you’ve recently faced. Write down how you felt at that moment, what was going through your mind, and how you reacted. Did you avoid the pain or face it head-on? Reflect on how your approach influenced the outcome and whether you could have made a different choice."

Part V: The Power of Silent Decisions

Part V: The Power of Silent Decisions

Not all choices are loud. Some are made in silence—in what we don't say, in the emotions we hide, in the reactions we suppress. Even silence holds power. Sometimes, it protects us. Sometimes, it limits us. In this part, we explore those quiet moments where choices happen internally, without the world noticing, but still shaping who we are becoming.

Chapter 11: The Space Between Reaction and Response

You Can Choose to Feel Pain or Choose to Let Go—Neither Is Wrong.

There's a silent space inside every situation—between what happens and how we respond. And in that space, there's a choice: to feel the pain fully or to let it go gently.

People often believe they must always be strong, that letting go is weakness or that holding onto pain makes them real. But both are valid. Both are choices. If you feel pain deeply, cry, or sit with it—there's no shame in that. And if you take a deep breath and decide to move on—there's strength in that **too.**

In my life, I've had moments where I chose to feel pain, let it burn, and stay with me. And in others, I let go before it grew heavy. Sometimes I wasn't ready to hold it. Sometimes I wasn't ready to release it. But each time,

I understood—there's no single right way. There's only your way.

What matters is being honest with yourself in that space between the moment and your response. Whether you choose to feel or to release, make that choice from awareness, not fear. From courage, not pressure.

That's where your power lives.

There are moments in life when pain knocks at your door, uninvited and heavy. And sometimes, we do let it in. We sit with it. We cry, reflect, and understand. Other times, we see the pain coming, acknowledge it, and quietly choose not to let it rule the moment.

I had a moment like that.

It was the night before my main exams. Everything I had studied for was resting on the next morning. But at midnight, I had a deep emotional fight with the one I love the most. My heart felt torn. And yet, I had to make a decision—not for him, not even against him, but for me.

I could have sat in that pain. I could have let it steal my sleep and fill my mind. But I chose otherwise. I closed my eyes, held space for my emotions, and whispered to myself, “This pain can wait. Right now, I choose me.” I woke up at 5 a.m. with clarity, studied, and gave my exam with focus.

That wasn’t the absence of love. That was a presence of self-respect. I didn’t stop loving him. He still means the world to me. But in that moment, I remembered—real love doesn’t mean forgetting yourself. It means carrying both love and self-awareness together.

That’s what emotional strength truly is. It’s not about being emotionless or unaffected. It’s about choosing the right emotion at the right time, for the right reason—especially when it’s hard.

So if you're ever stuck between love and responsibility, pain and peace—remember this: You can choose to feel pain, and you can choose to let go. Neither is wrong. What matters is that you choose with honesty and for your own growth.

Not Every Feeling Needs to Be Fixed; Some Just Need to Be Felt

In our daily life, we're conditioned to solve emotions like problems. If we're sad, we try to cheer up. If we're angry, we try to cool down. If someone else is crying, we rush to say "Don't cry" instead of letting them cry. But feelings aren't always puzzles to solve—sometimes, they're just experiences that want to pass through us.

I've had days when I felt low without any strong reason. I didn't have a heartbreak, I didn't fail in anything, and I wasn't even physically tired. But there was this silent heaviness sitting inside me. Earlier, I used to panic. I'd ask myself, "Why am I feeling like this?", "How do I fix this?" I'd talk to people, overthink, distract myself, or even fake smiles.

But now I've learned: some feelings are not meant to be escaped or solved. They are just there to be felt.

One evening, I just allowed myself to sit with the silence inside me. No music. No scrolling. No distractions. Just me and that unexplainable emotion. I didn't label it. I didn't run away from it. I let it be. After a while, I felt a calmness I hadn't known before. That moment taught me something important:

The body feels what it needs to feel. The soul doesn't need a solution—it needs your presence

We often confuse healing with fixing. But real healing starts when you stop fighting every emotion and start honouring it.

So next time you feel something strange or heavy—don't rush to fix it. Maybe all it needs... ...is for you to say, "Hey, I see you. Stay for a while, if you must."

In relationships, all someone often needs is a person who can listen and help them heal, not necessarily solve their problems. When someone shares their struggles, they don't always want immediate solutions—they just want to be heard. Offering advice too quickly can make them feel like their emotions are being brushed aside. Choose to hear before you suggest. By simply being present and allowing them to express themselves, you create a space for healing. In doing so, you show empathy and support, making it easier for them to open up when they're ready to address their issues.

You don’t have to dwell—you can move when you’re ready

"You don’t have to dwell—you can move when you’re ready" emphasizes the importance of personal timing in healing and growth. It's easy to feel rushed by others' expectations to move on from pain, but true progress comes when you're ready. It's okay to take the time you need to process your emotions before moving forward. Healing isn't linear, and forcing yourself to move on too soon can prevent genuine emotional growth. The power lies in recognizing when you're ready to take the next step on your own terms.

During my college days, a friend of mine confessed that he loved me. I didn’t feel the same, but I respected his feelings deeply. I told him no—gently, honestly—but he didn’t stop.

His friends joined in, pressuring me with questions:

“Why not?”
“What’s wrong with him?”
“Just agree—he’s a good person.”

What they didn’t understand was that love isn't a favour you return. It’s a choice.
And I was tired.

Tired of explaining myself. Tired of being questioned for saying no to something I didn’t feel.

For a while, I was emotionally disturbed. I began to question myself, too—**Was I wrong? Was I selfish? Should I give in just to stop the conflict?**

But then I paused. I breathed. And I chose myself.

I walked away from those friendships, not with hate, but with peace. I didn't rush to replace them. I didn't force myself to be okay overnight. I took time to work on myself. Slowly, I found clarity, strength, and calm.

Now, when I look back, I don't regret that decision.
Because I moved when **I was ready**.
Not when they wanted me to.
Not when I felt guilty.
Not to please anyone.

Just because I knew deep inside, it was time.

Chapter 12: The Pause Between Feeling and Action

This topic highlights the crucial space between feeling and reacting. It encourages us to take a moment, pause, and reflect before responding to a situation. Often, we get caught up in our emotions, reacting impulsively without considering the consequences or the most thoughtful response. However, by creating this pause, we allow ourselves to choose how we want to respond, rather than letting our immediate feelings dictate our actions.

This space is sacred because it allows us to act consciously, in alignment with our true intentions, rather than reacting out of anger, fear, or impulsivity. It empowers us to respond thoughtfully and to approach challenges with emotional awareness and maturity.

Pause, Think, respond — A Sacred Space Exists Before Reaction

In our fast-paced lives, it's easy to get caught up in the whirlwind of emotions and rush into reactions. Whether it's a heated argument, a moment of frustration, or a situation that triggers an emotional response, our natural instinct is often to react immediately. But what if we took a step back before we acted? This is the power of the pause.

The pause is the space between feeling and action — the moment we give ourselves before responding. It's not about ignoring or suppressing our emotions, but rather about recognizing them and choosing how we want to express them. In that pause, we gain the freedom to reflect on our emotions, assess the situation, and decide on the best way to respond. This allows us to act more thoughtfully and with intention, rather than simply reacting out of habit or impulse.

The pause is the space between feeling and action — the moment we give ourselves before responding. It's not about ignoring or suppressing our emotions, but rather about recognizing them and choosing how we want to express them. In that pause, we gain the freedom to reflect on our emotions, assess the situation, and decide on the best way to respond. This allows us to act more thoughtfully and with intention, rather than simply reacting out of habit or impulse.

For example,

If someone says something hurtful to us, our initial feeling may be anger. But if we take a moment to pause, we might realize that reacting with anger won't help the situation.

Instead, we can choose to respond with understanding or assertiveness, expressing our feelings calmly rather than letting our emotions control us.

This pause is sacred because it's where we make conscious choices. It's where we hold power over our actions, and it's the key to cultivating emotional maturity. Rather than getting trapped in the cycle of emotional reactions, we can move forward in a more grounded, balanced, and intentional way.

Giving yourself a moment can change what you carry forever

We often underestimate the power of a single pause. In life, it's not just the major events that shape us — it's how we respond in small, emotional moments. Giving yourself one moment of silence, one deep breath before speaking, or one beat of reflection before reacting can change what stays with you forever.

It's not about avoiding feelings. It's about making space to choose — to choose what kind of person you want to be in that moment.

A Real-Life Reflection

I still remember a moment from my own life — it was during a tough conversation with someone close to me. They said something that triggered me deeply. My first instinct was to argue, defend, and throw words in return that I would regret. But something in me paused. I just went quiet — not because I had nothing to say, but because I realized I didn't want to carry the burden of that reaction.

That pause gave me time to really feel what I was experiencing — hurt, confusion, and a craving to be heard, not to fight. That single breath shifted the outcome. I responded gently instead of emotionally, and that moment healed instead of breaking. Had I spoken in that heat, I would've carried guilt, regret, and distance. But because I paused, I walked away with clarity, self-respect, and peace.

A pause is not a weakness. It's power.

In that pause, you don't lose control — you gain yourself. And sometimes, giving yourself a moment doesn't just change the moment.

it changes what your heart has to carry for a lifetime.

Daily Reflection Exercise: "Each evening, take five minutes to reflect on your day. Write down one instance where you responded instead of reacting. What was the situation? What did you feel? How did your decision impact your emotions and your relationships? This practice will help you strengthen your ability to pause before reacting in the future."

Part VI: Becoming a Person of Choice

Part VI: Becoming a Person of Choice

You don't need to be perfect. You only need to be present with awareness, truth, and freedom.

This part of the journey is not about becoming someone new—it's about finally being who you are, without the noise of fear, masks, or borrowed expectations. A "Person of Choice" isn't someone who always chooses correctly, but someone who chooses consciously. Someone who pauses, feels, questions, and then acts from a place of clarity.

It's about standing in your truth, knowing that presence matters more than perfection. And most of all, it's about permitting yourself to live honestly, even if the world around you prefers performance.

Chapter 13: You Are the One Who Decides

Your Thinking is Yours

In the end, no matter how many emotions we feel, how many masks we wear, or how many paths we explore in love, pain, and healing — the one thing that stays with us is our own mind.

Your thoughts are yours.

Your choices are yours.

Even silence is yours.

We often think circumstances decide for us. Or we wait for people to validate what we already know deep inside. But the moment you realize that your thinking — your interpretations, beliefs, and mental choices — belong to you, something shifts. You become not a victim of life but a creator of it.

Whether it's:

- choosing peace over proving,
- choosing honesty over a polished image,
- or choosing to pause instead of react.

It all starts with the way you think.

This chapter is your reminder: no matter what happened in the past or what confusion you're in now — you are still the one who decides what to carry, what to let go, and what to become.

Your Emotions Are Yours

Your emotions are not something that "happens" to you — they rise within you.

Yes, people may trigger something. Situations may stir waves inside you. But the storm or calm that follows? That's yours. It belongs to your inner world, your past, your stories, your values.

Often, we say:

- “He made me angry.”
- “She broke me.”
- “That situation ruined my peace.”

But if we take a pause and look deeper — no one can make us feel anything unless it already had a place inside us.

This isn’t blame. This is freedom.

Because if our emotions are ours, we are no longer puppets. We’re artists — sculpting how we respond, grow, and heal.

I once thought emotional pain meant weakness. I avoided it, tried to push it away. But slowly I realized: Owning your emotions — even the uncomfortable ones — is the bravest thing you can do. It’s where healing begins. It’s where self-respect deepens.

So feel your feelings. Don’t outsource your emotional reality. It’s okay to cry, to be angry, to be joyful, to be confused.

But own it.

Name it.

Sit with it.

And then, choose what to do with it.

Because they're yours. And you are the one who decides what story they tell.

Your Life Is Yours — and That's Your Strength

From the moment you wake up to the moment you sleep, you are living your life, not your parents', not your partner's, not society's. Yours.

But here's the twist:

Many of us live as if we owe every decision to someone else's expectation.

We follow paths we didn't choose.

We say yes when we want to scream no.

We stay silent when our hearts are begging to speak.

And all the while, we quietly carry a weight — the weight of a life unlived.

But here's the truth I learned, sometimes painfully: No one is coming to choose for you. No one will fully understand your feelings, your fears, your hopes. That's not their fault — it's simply because they're not you.

So if your life is yours, let that become your power

Even if you’ve made mistakes. Even if you’ve been hurt. Even if others tried to write your story, you still get to pick up the pen.

I had moments where I blamed others for where I stood. But once I began owning the smallest of choices —

What I said,

What I allowed,

WI believed.

I felt free.

Not perfectly free. But genuinely strong. And that’s where real strength lies: In not outsourcing your life.

In showing up, knowing this is your road, and walking it.

Not to prove anything. Not to please anyone. But to live a life you can respect when you're alone with yourself.

Chapter 14: The Return to Self

Everything we explored—emotions, truth, silence, awareness, love—was never about changing who we are. It was always about returning to who we've always been underneath the noise.

This chapter is a gentle homecoming. After all the reflections, stories, and choices we've walked through, it's time to look within and say:

"I am not broken. I am becoming."

We've unlearned illusions.

We've learned the power of awareness.

Now, we return—not to the old self, but to the real one.

Let's explore this together.

Let Life Be Simple: Feel, Reflect, Choose

Growth isn't always about giant leaps. Sometimes, it's in the quiet, everyday choices you make.

Choose to wake up early—not to impress, but to honour the stillness.

Choose to wake up with a smile—not because everything is perfect, but because you're willing to begin.

Choose to cook for yourself—not because you must, but because you matter.

Choose to walk with nature—not as an escape, but as a return.

Choose to sit with your family—not out of duty, but out of presence.

Choose to clean your space—not for the world to see, but for your soul to breathe.

These are not just routines. They are micro-decisions of self-love. They are not signs that you're changing—they are proof that you're choosing.

And in those choices, you are slowly, steadily, becoming.

These are not the things that need changing. These are choices for building yourself.

Morning Reflection Ritual: "Start each day with a simple ritual. When you wake up, spend a few minutes in silence. Ask yourself: 'What is the intention I want to set for today?' It could be as simple as choosing to be present, kind, or grateful. This small habit will anchor your day in intention, helping you make more conscious choices throughout."

Come Back to Yourself, Again and Again

It's easy to think that the journey of life should be one continuous upward climb—without obstacles or disappointments. But the truth is, we all experience setbacks. We make choices, we pursue dreams, we fall in love—and sometimes, the outcomes aren't what we expected. It's in these moments that we're tempted to question ourselves, doubt our path, or even give up. But this is where the real growth begins: not in avoiding failure, but in choosing to come back to yourself when things don't go as planned.

I've found that the moments I've faced the greatest disappointment were the same moments that taught me the most about who I am. Love doesn't always go as we hope; dreams may feel far away. But each time we experience these setbacks, we are presented with a choice: to stay down or to rise again. To choose ourselves, to reflect, to learn, and to choose again.

Coming back to yourself doesn't mean pretending everything is okay when it's not. It means allowing yourself to feel, reflect on what happened, and then decide to keep moving forward— no matter how many times it takes. The key to resilience isn't in never falling; it's in getting back up each time, stronger and more aware of your own power.

So, whenever you find yourself doubting your worth, feeling like you've failed, or just feeling lost, remember: you can always come back to yourself. The ups and downs are not the end; they are part of the process. Choosing to start again, to learn from each experience, and to trust in your ability to keep moving forward—this is the real strength.

This is Not About Control. It's About Inner Freedom

This book isn't about telling you what to do, how to act, or what choices to make. It's not a manual with steps to follow or a formula for success. It's not about me telling you to change this or fix that. You see, I've realized that life isn't about control—it's about freedom. The freedom to choose how we respond, to choose who we want to be, and to choose how we want to live each day.

I've learned that true freedom comes when I stop trying to control everything around me. Life is unpredictable, and it's impossible to control every single moment. There's beauty in that unpredictability. We can't control what happens to us, but we can choose how we respond. That's where the power lies. I've stopped forcing myself to fit into a box, to meet expectations, or to chase some ideal version of perfection. Instead, I've embraced the freedom to just be.

This journey isn't about managing everything in my life. It's about accepting the ups and downs, the chaos and calm, and realizing that I don't have to be perfect. I'm not here to control the outcome, but I am here to choose what feels right for me, in the moment. I've come to understand that freedom means choosing to live authentically, to embrace my emotions, to let go of what no longer serves me, and to make choices that align with the person I want to become.

When I chose to let go of control, I found that I was no longer bound by fear or expectations. I started to listen to myself more deeply, to make decisions that were true to my heart, and to let life unfold without resistance. Freedom isn't about being flawless—it's about being real, about showing up as who you truly are.

This isn't about telling you how to do anything. This is about encouraging you to give yourself the freedom to choose, to feel, to make mistakes, and to grow in your own unique way. Your life, your choices, your path—they're all yours to create. And that, my friend, is where your true power lies.

Final Reflection: "Now that you've explored the concept of choice and awareness, take a moment to reflect on how your perspective has shifted. How has your understanding of choice in love, relationships, and self-awareness changed over the course of this book? What is one action you will commit to taking from this point forward to live as a person of choice?"

“Becoming a person of choice” never ends. It's an ongoing process of self-discovery, growth, and alignment with one's true self.

Conclusion

You Were Always Free

We grow up believing that life happens to us. That emotions just arrive, that love controls us, that strength means silence, and that being good means being liked. But the truth is softer—and far more powerful.

You were never meant to perform a version of yourself to be accepted.

You were never meant to carry emotions that aren't yours.

You were never meant to stay silent to seem strong.

You were never meant to live by assumptions and call it reality.

This book wasn't written to fix you, because you were never broken. It was written to remind you: you have a choice.

A choice to feel honestly.

A choice to speak with presence.

A choice to pause, reflect, and respond.

A choice to love, to leave, to begin again.

And the most sacred choice of all—the choice to be yourself.

You are not just the sum of your thoughts or your pain.

You are the one who sees them. You are awareness. You are love.

You are the choice.

Walk out of these pages knowing:

You are allowed to choose differently at any moment.

That's not just freedom.

That's power.

That's peace.

Closing Note to the Reader

You've just read a book that doesn't ask you to change who you are—it asks you to remember who you are beneath the noise, beneath the pressure, beneath the masks.

Every page was written not to give you rules, but to remind you that you have a choice—to feel, to pause, to respond, to show up, to walk away, to stay soft, to be bold.

There's no single right way to live. There is only your way—guided by awareness, not assumptions.

So whenever life asks you to react, remember: ✧ Pause. Think. Choose.

✧ **Feel fully. Then move freely.**

✧ **Live a life where assumptions don't overrule you.**

You are a person of choice. With love and truth, Divya Madhabattula

Acknowledgments

I would like to extend my sincere gratitude to **Aarav** for being an invaluable source of guidance and support throughout the creation of this book. Your insightful advice and assistance have helped me shape my ideas and structure this work in ways I never imagined. Thank you for being with me every step of the way.

About the Author

I'm **Divya Madhabattula**, a deeply reflective thinker and an explorer of emotional truth. I believe that every feeling, every response, and every moment is a choice, and through this book, I want to help people realize that they can choose clarity over confusion and courage over emotional silence.

People of Choice is my invitation to you: to break free from the emotional performances we've been taught and begin living from a place of honesty, not habit. My words come from lived experiences, quiet observations, and a lifelong search for meaning beneath the surface.

When I'm not writing, I spend my time reflecting, understanding people, and seeking strength in awareness. I believe awareness is the real freedom, and we all deserve to live from that place.

To live clearly, you must first choose to see honestly.

www.ingramcontent.com/pod-product-compliance
Lightning Source LLC
Chambersburg PA
CBHW062143160726
48282CB00027B/927
9789334306699